Set Sail

On Your Leadership Journey

A JOURNAL OF SELF-DISCOVERY

Amy Leneker

> **IN THE JOURNAL
> I DO NOT JUST EXPRESS
> MYSELF MORE OPENLY
> THAN I COULD TO ANY PERSON;
> I CREATE MYSELF.**
>
> **SUSAN SONTAG**

Set Sail on Your Leadership Journey: A Journal of Self-Discovery
Copyright © 2018 by Amy Leneker
All rights reserved

No part of this book may be used or reproduced in any form without the written permission of the author.

www.AmyLeneker.com

ISBN 978-1-7328458-1-7

Cover and book design by Debi Bodett
www.DebiBodett.com

Printed in the United States of America

Published by Amy Leneker
Olympia, Washington

Introduction

My love affair with the ocean began the moment I first saw it. It was an affair that would last a lifetime. As decades came and went, I continued to seek the solace of the saltwater air. When I am near the ocean, I feel alive, and hopeful and free.

My love affair with leadership was not quite as romantic. As I climbed the career ladder, my leadership responsibilities continued to increase. And so did my anxiety. I was overwhelmed, exhausted and confused. If I finally had the job I'd worked so hard to get why was I so miserable?

What followed was a soul-searching, gut wrenching journey to get clear about what I really wanted to do. And more importantly, who did I want to be? Those were the questions I had been afraid to ask, because deep down I knew the answers. I had always known.

The book you're holding in your hands is intended to help you discover what you already know. What you've always known. My hope for you is that you follow your heart and that it leads you to what makes you feel alive, and hopeful and free.

Amy Leneker

THE BEST WAY TO PREDICT THE FUTURE IS TO CREATE IT.

PETER DRUCKER
MANAGEMENT CONSULTANT AND AUTHOR

What do you want your future to look like?
Write uninterrupted for five minutes.
You may be surprised at what you discover.

> A SMOOTH SEA NEVER MADE A SKILLED SAILOR.
>
> — FRANKLIN D. ROOSEVELT

Describe a challenge you encountered during the last year.

How did you overcome it?

> A CALM AND MODEST LIFE
> BRINGS MORE HAPPINESS
> THAN THE PURSUIT OF SUCCESS
> COMBINED WITH CONSTANT RELENTLESSNESS.
>
> ALBERT EINSTEIN

What 3 things make your soul wildly happy?

1. _____

2. _____

3. _____

How will you choose to show up as a leader in your life today?

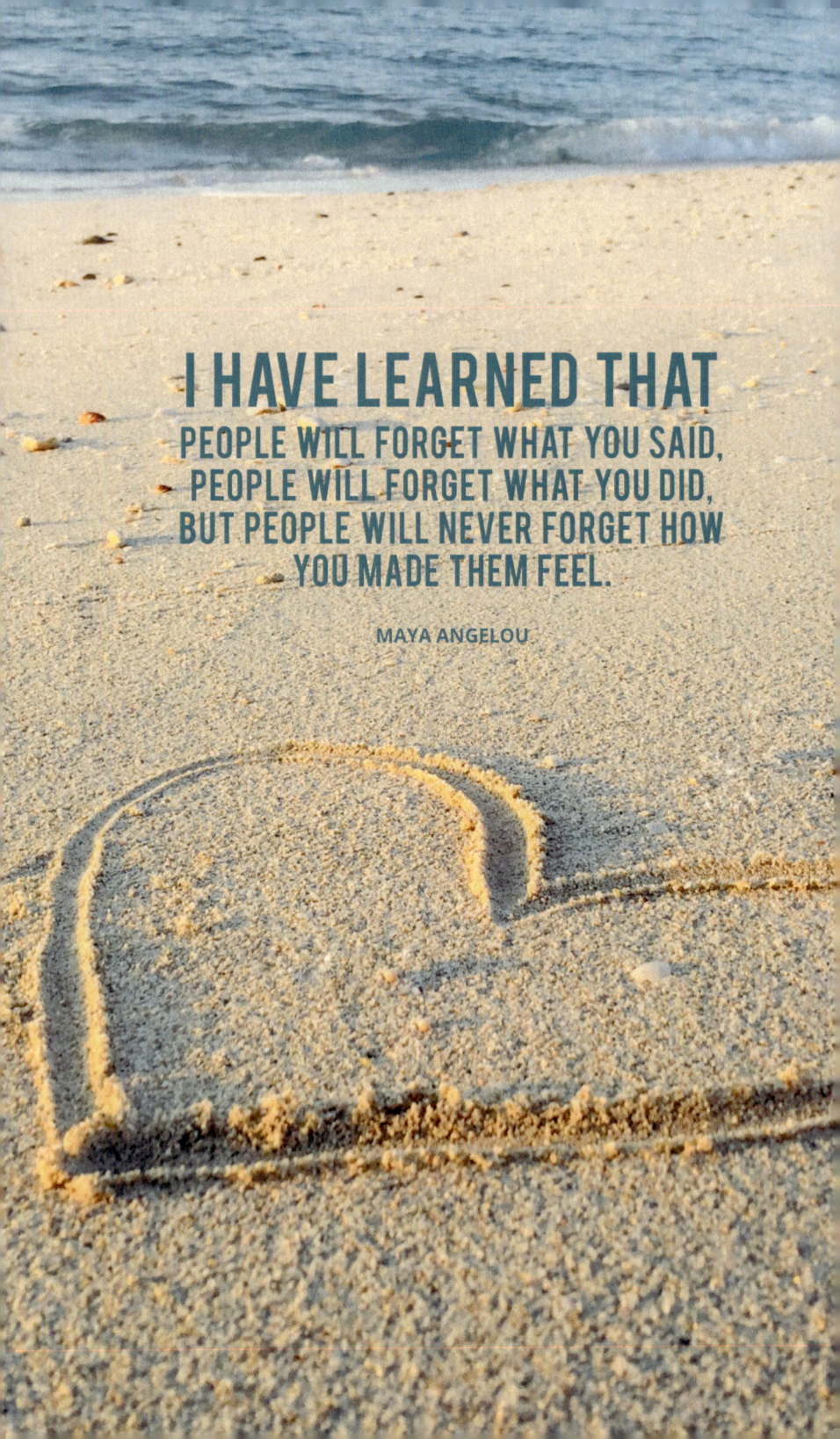

Think of a leader who has had a positive impact on your life.
Write their name here.

_____

How did that person make you feel?
Circle your answers.

TRUSTED   SUPPORTED   SPECIAL   SMART

COMPETENT   PROFESSIONAL   VALUED

CARED FOR   LOVED   SAFE   SECURE

HOPEFUL   JOYFUL   HAPPY   OPTIMISTIC

CREATIVE   INNOVATIVE   RESPECTED

CONFIDENT   SUCCESSFUL

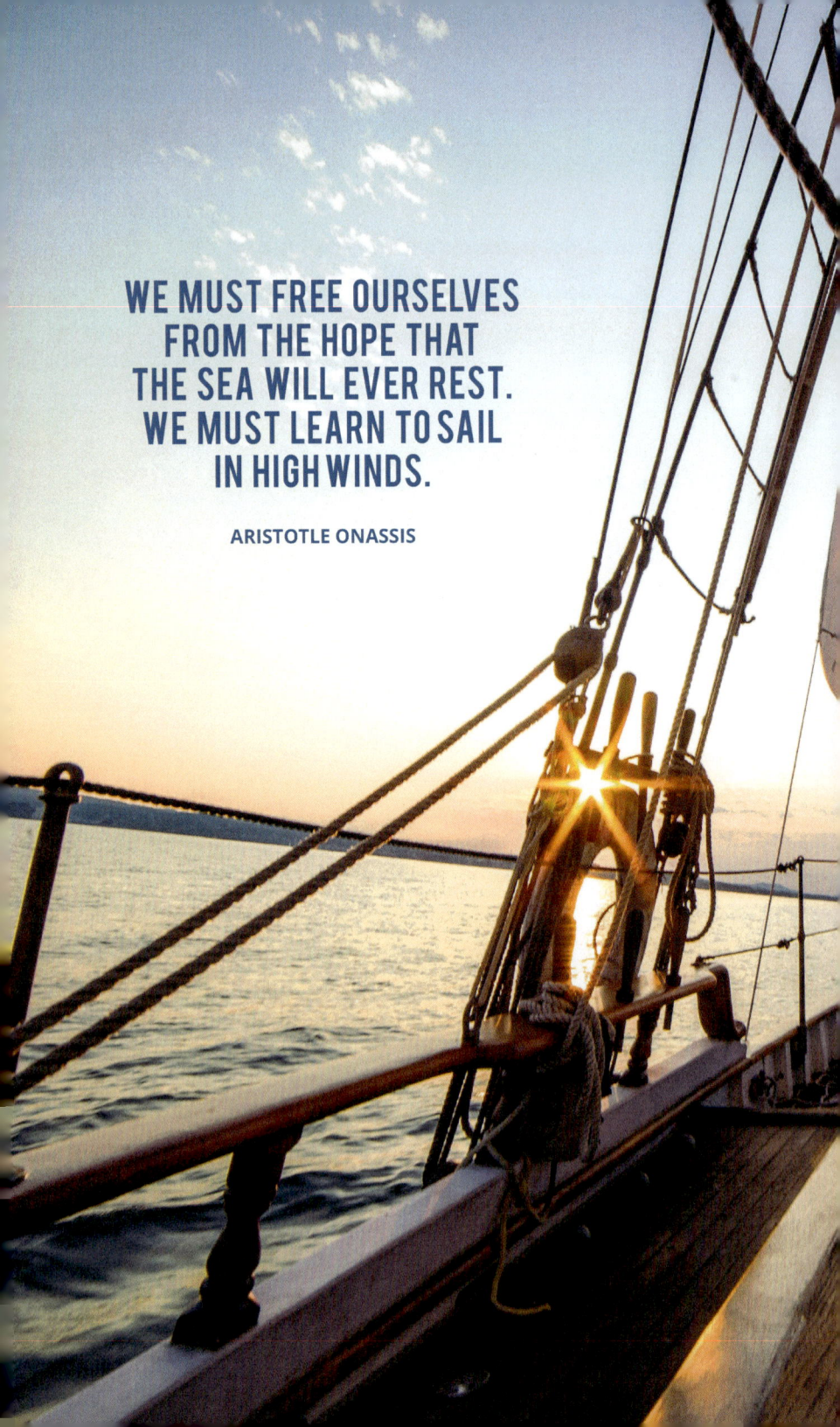

What are you waiting for?

Joy and happiness are too important to be delayed.
Rather than waiting for the perfect conditions
in which to find joy or happiness, feel them today.
Write as many things as you can that bring you joy.

1. _____
2. _____
3. _____
4. _____
5. _____
6. _____
7. _____
8. _____
9. _____
10. _____

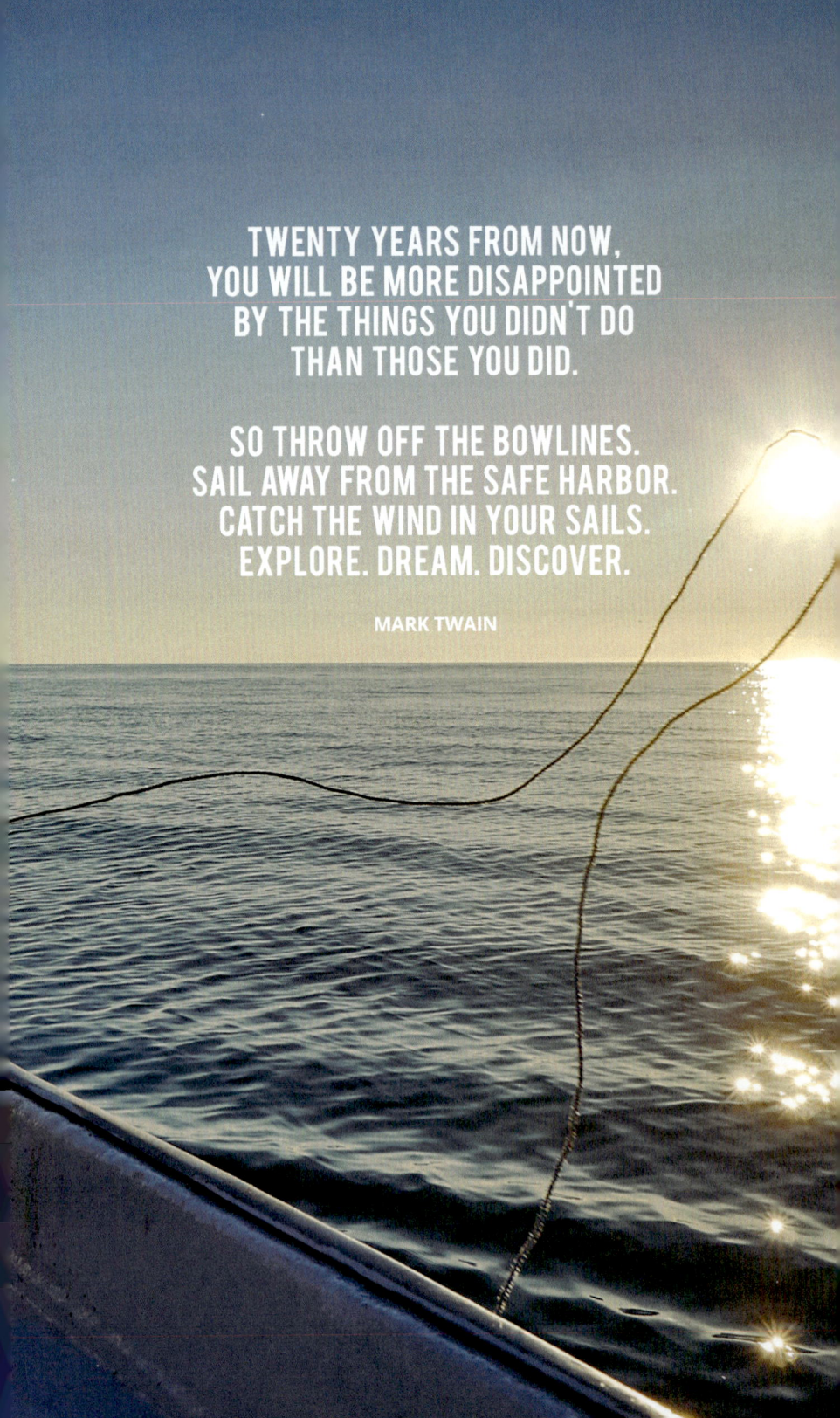

What do these 3 words mean to you?

Quiet your mind and listen to your heart as you complete the sentences below. Be still and wait for the answers to come.

I want to explore...

_____

_____

_____

I dream of...

_____

_____

_____

I want to discover...

_____

_____

_____

Have you ever "lost yourself" in work or a relationship?
What did you do to find yourself again?

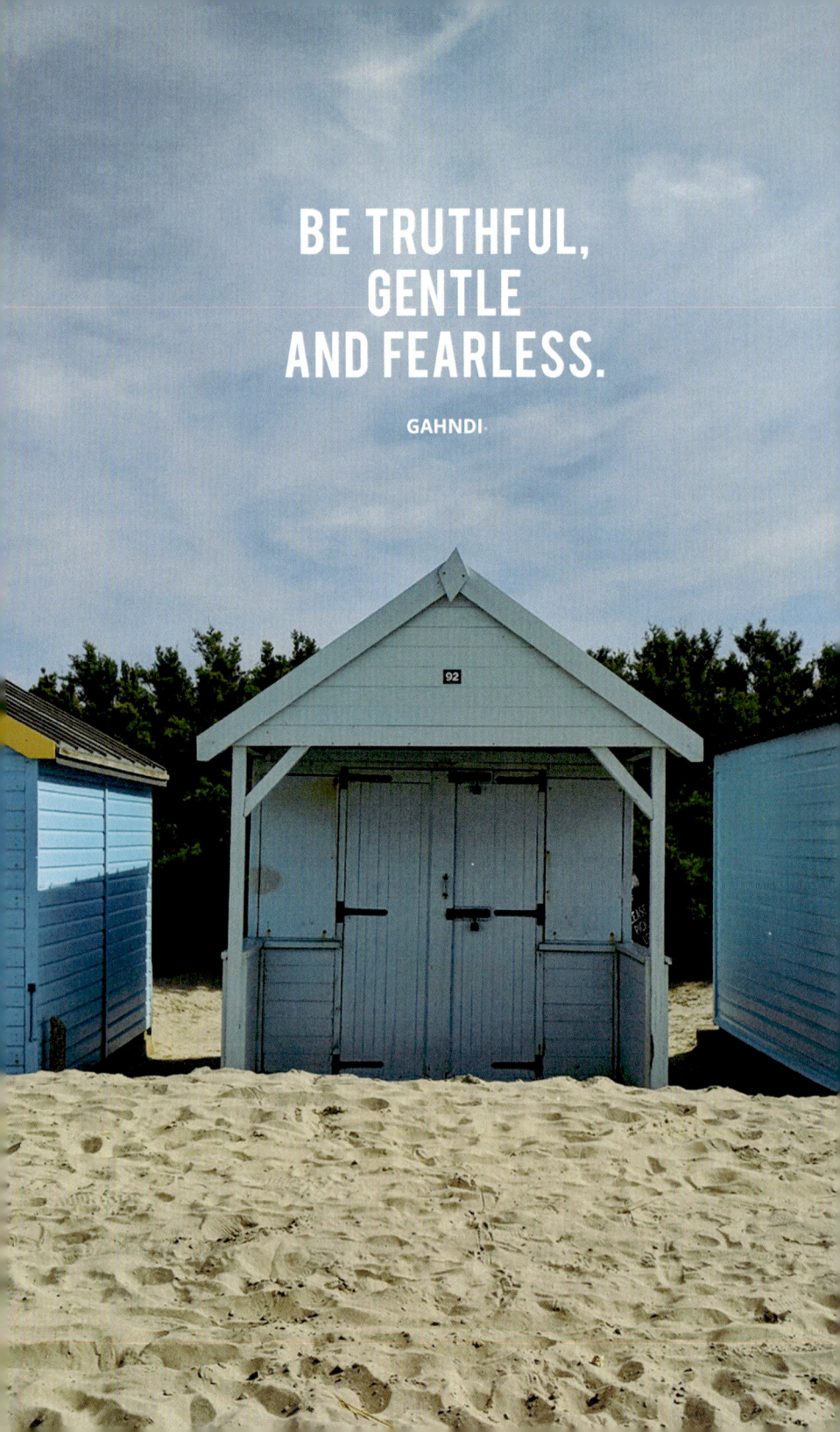

Describe a time today when you were...

Truthful

Gentle

Fearless

What is one thing you would do if you weren't afraid?

What is something you've always wanted to learn and why?

WE OURSELVES FEEL
THAT WHAT WE ARE DOING
IS JUST A DROP IN THE OCEAN.

BUT THE OCEAN WOULD BE LESS
BECAUSE OF THAT MISSING DROP.

MOTHER TERESA

When you reflect on your life thus far, what is something you're proud of?

The saying goes that we become like the five people we spend the most time with.

With whom are you spending your time?

1. _____

2. _____

3. _____

4. _____

5. _____

The best leaders see in us what we can't see in ourselves.

Describe a leader that has had a positive impact on your life. What did they see in you that you weren't ready to see in yourself?

_____

_____

_____

_____

_____

_____

_____

_____

HAVE THE COURAGE TO FOLLOW
YOUR HEART AND INTUITION.
THEY SOMEHOW ALREADY KNOW
WHAT YOU TRULY WANT TO BECOME.

STEVE JOBS

If you were to follow your heart and intuition, where would they lead you?

*Your values are at the core of who you are.
Values are what you stand for.*

Check your top 5 values from the list below.
If you don't see the word you're looking for, add it to the list.

Abundance	Excellence	Love
Accountability	Fairness	Money
Achievement	Faith	Nature
Action	Family	Passion
Adventure	Flexibility	Peace
Balance	Freedom	Perfection
Beauty	Friendship	Philanthropy
Calmness	Fulfilment	Power
Clarity	Fun	Respect
Comfort	Harmony	Security
Compassion	Happiness	Simplicity
Competition	Health	Significance
Connection	Honesty	Spirituality
Contribution	Honor	Spontaneity
Courage	Humility	Strength
Creativity	Independence	Stability
Curiosity	Integrity	Success
Determination	Intelligence	Teamwork
Discipline	Intimacy	Tolerance
Effectiveness	Inspiration	Tradition
Empathy	Kindness	Truth
Energy	Knowledge	Wealth
Enthusiasm	Liveliness	Wisdom

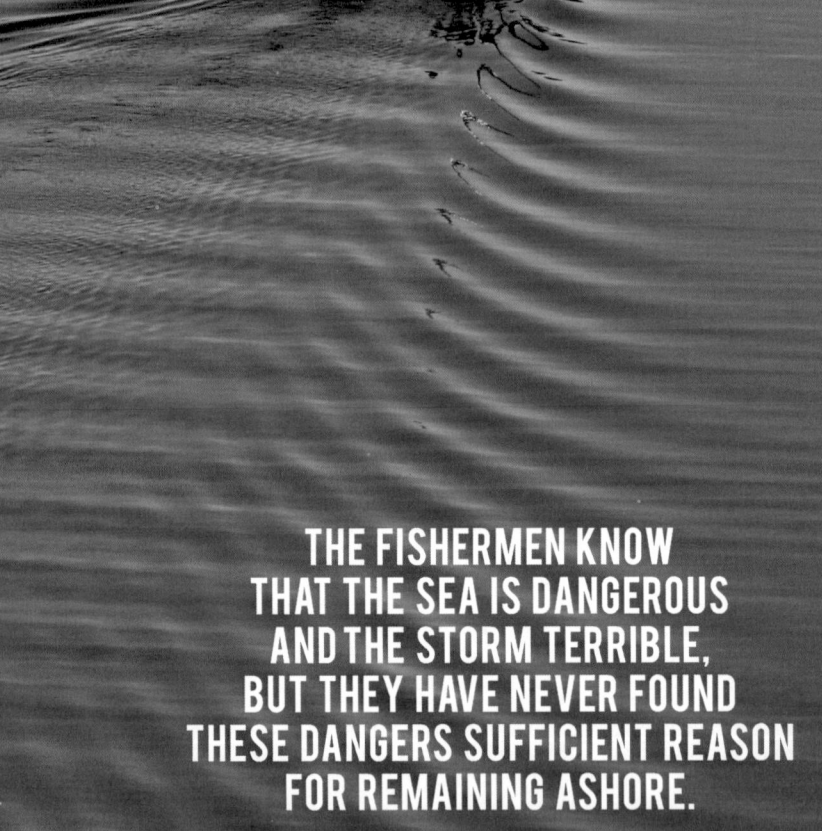

What are you afraid to do?
If your best friend were afraid of the same thing, what encouraging words would you share?

Write them here.
And then say them to yourself!

_____

_____

_____

_____

_____

_____

_____

_____

Rate yourself on the following scales.

Micromanage   Give lots of freedom

⭐ ⭐ ⭐ ⭐ ⭐ ⭐ ⭐ ⭐ ⭐ ⭐

Explain how something   Explain why something
needs to be done   needs to be done

⭐ ⭐ ⭐ ⭐ ⭐ ⭐ ⭐ ⭐ ⭐ ⭐

Talk about what   Ask about what
motivates me   motivates others

⭐ ⭐ ⭐ ⭐ ⭐ ⭐ ⭐ ⭐ ⭐ ⭐

Focus on failures   Celebrate successes

⭐ ⭐ ⭐ ⭐ ⭐ ⭐ ⭐ ⭐ ⭐ ⭐

> **WITHOUT GOALS, AND PLANS TO REACH THEM, YOU ARE LIKE A SHIP THAT HAS SET SAIL WITH NO DESTINATION.**
>
> FITZHUGH DODSON

What is a goal you would like to accomplish in the next year?

Draw your leadership journey on the timeline below.

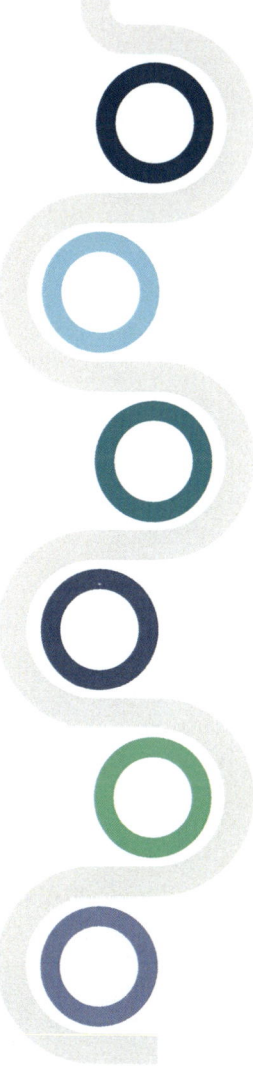

> **TO BE SUCCESSFUL AT SEA
> WE MUST KEEP THINGS SIMPLE.**
>
> PETE CULLER

What are 3 things you could do to simplify your life?

1. _____

2. _____

3. _____

Draw a picture or write a poem to describe what leadership means to you.

When you think about what makes you feel alive and full of purpose, how would you complete this sentence?

I cannot not...

What could you start, stop and continue doing to move in the direction of your dreams?

Start...

Stop...

Continue...

If your soul had a song, what would it be?

Is there an area in your life where you feel stuck? How can you get "unstuck"?

How flexible are you?
Rate yourself on the scale below.

Not flexible   Very flexible

①   ②   ③   ④   ⑤

What could you do to be more flexible?

_____

_____

_____

_____

_____

_____

_____

What is it that you are built for?
What is your heart's purpose?

Challenge yourself to do one thing every day this week that scares you.
Just think of how proud you'll feel!

Monday

Tuesday

Wednesday

Thursday

Friday

Saturday

Sunday

Imagine you had an entire day to spend however you choose.

What would you do?

_____

_____

_____

_____

What would it take to make this dream day a reality?

_____

_____

_____

_____

Have you been waiting for someone to change your life?

The person who can change your life is you.
What would you like to change?

_____

_____

_____

_____

_____

_____

_____

_____

_____

Notes

Made in the USA
Middletown, DE
22 November 2018